Praise for *Hard Listening*

"Alison Luterman is one of my favorite poetic voices. I eat her poetry like buttered bread and it goes straight into my depleted spiritual bloodstream. The poems in this collection are luminous. They are wise without being preachy, funny and heartbreakingly real, distilled to quintessence, grounded in everyday realities that welcome her readers home to the sacred ground of their own lives. Her conversations with deceased musicians are extraordinary! I felt like I was glimpsing an intimate dance between women on opposite sides of the veil."

— Mirabai Starr, author of *Wild Mercy, Living the Fierce and Tender Mercy of the Women Mystics*

"Alison Luterman somehow manages to give us hope in this nearly hopeless time, encouragement when we can barely get up in the morning, laughter and beauty when everything otherwise seems glum and dark. She sings the song of an America for which we almost forgot the lyrics and can barely recall the tune, but it lifts and consoles us. Thank you, Alison."

— Robert Reich, professor at UC Berkeley and former United States Secretary of Labor. Author of many books including *The System: Who Rigged It, How We Fix It*

"In this engaging homage to listening, Alison Luterman honors iconic singers from Odetta to Amy Winehouse to Barbra Streisand. We are invited into the suffering and talent of the greats: 'that throb, that ache, that ascent of flying doves / over city rooftops.' Narrative poems detail the lives, voices, and music of women whose style and personal grit have inspired the speaker to find her own voice in poetry and song. In richly varied syntax, she juxtaposes aging and learning–the admiration of many voices and the hard work of developing one's own. Luterman embraces becoming 'someone / hollowed-out enough to listen' with warm authenticity. Despite the challenges of pandemic and politics, there is a harmony revealed in *Hard Listening*: we can survive hardship. We can explore aging and partnering with grace and passion–'Because this kind of truth lives on and on– / it is made of silver / and light / and bone.'"

— Ellen Bass, author of nine poetry collections, most recently *Indigo*

"Equal parts dazzling and gritty. God, I love these poems. They're open-throated. Funny. Fierce. Wise. They make me fall more deeply in love with the whole of life, its shit and its brilliance. Here, Alison Luterman finds music in everyday moments—losing an earring, making biscuits, changing in a locker room—and braids them with portraits of women singers and the ongoing story of her own learning to sing. She turns all into resonance. To read *Hard Listening* is to feel struck by the tuning fork of life, to vibrate with our own astonishing humanity, to be led toward an honest and humbling beauty."
  — Rosemerry Wahtola Trommer, author of *The Unfolding* and host of
    The Poetic Path

"Alison Luterman praises the insatiable divas: Janis, Ella, Billie, Nina, Joni, Aretha, and the many Ukrainian women keening as they sweep up broken glass. The poet joins her idols, singing and regretting and plunging forward in a wild vibrato deepened by age. This is a book about the broken promises of America and the incongruity of tradition, a fear of being in the wrong life on the wrong path that turns out to be the right path after all. It is a book about being dragged wisecracking into a sense of the larger meaning of it all.
  — Michael Simms, author of *Jubal Rising: Poems*

"I never know where I'm going to end up when I enter an Alison Luterman poem, but I always strap in, ready for a wild, illuminating, compassionate ride through the 'messy beauty' of daily life. Whether writing of a pair of pink suede boots that somehow "outlasted a cross-country move, / a starter marriage, and a few bouts of plantar fasciitis," or describing the unlikely joy of 'how many things I've been wrong about,' Luterman fills this new volume with her trademark humility and brash yet tender truths, exploring the ways we all 'still work to/hear the wounds under the words ... To listen / purely ... quivering with attention.'"
  — James Crews, author of *Turning Toward Grief: Reflections on Life, Loss,*
    and Appreciation

"These poems are at home in the world, adept in moments—a walk around the lake with a friend, singing in the basement with a spouse, waiting for a loved-one in surgery. Luterman is a poet who rests in the complex jumble of the human, in words, 'compressed to diamonds by the weight of love and time.'"
  — Danusha Lameris, author of *Bonfire Opera* and *Blade by Blade*

HARD
LISTENING

poems

Alison Luterman

Wildhouse
Poetry

For my song-making collaborators:
Lee Bates, Steve Chiasson, Jen Coogan, Loren Linnard,
Sheela Ramesh, and especially Richard Jennings for
his brilliance, kindness, and endless patience in
teaching me to sing.

Contents

III / Snowy Plovers

ACCESS ROAD

I don't know if other people feel like there's a life
running alongside their so-called real life
like an access road runs alongside the main highway.
It's funkier, lonelier; you didn't expect to find yourself
on this one-lane frontage path, you kept thinking
you'd get on the freeway any minute now,
where you fondly imagined yourself
doing eighty, ninety, hurtling down
the untrammeled autobahn of free will.
That was the life you thought would be yours
when you were young and everything seemed laid out
as at a picnic with red gingham tablecloths.
But in your fantasies you neglected to factor in the ants
crawling up your legs,
the way they tickle and sting,
or the spilled juice and crumbled potato chips,
and your beautiful mother young again, and strong,
yet anxious and discontent amid all that messy beauty
because she, too, was always calibrating
how reality didn't measure up to the story.
So you've inherited her dilemma, what else is new,
and evening is drawing nigh, and you are still
on that access road, which as it turns out
is going to the same place
the main road was headed all along.

I

Season of the Sonnets

GHOSTS

None of the ones I ever asked
to haunt me have shown up,
except, very occasionally, in dreams,
though my sister-in-law *swears* my dead mother
appeared at the bird feeder one day as a red cardinal
looking straight at her with piercing eyes.
I asked Carla, when she was dying,
to give me a sign from the other side
if she could, and she snorted
because she didn't believe in any of that shit,
and sure enough, radio silence on her end,
eleven years now. I did hear a ghostly rustling
and creaking all night in an old pre-war
apartment building in Paris
when I was twenty, sleeping on a stranger's couch.
Hidden Jews still whispering in the closets,
or just wind and wood?
In Peru once, at an ancient Incan site
where maidens had been sacrificed, I burst
into unexpected tears as if some part of me
remembered something unnamable.
And once, when I was eighteen, on a tiny island
off the coast of Maine, all alone
for three days, foraging for berries
and very hungry, I sat on a rock, blinking in and out
like a strobe light, receiving signals
from the ether, eavesdropping
on strangers' conversations—though there was no one
to be seen, not even a deer. My dreams
those three days were mostly of ice cream,
the longing so intense I could taste it. But I never knew,
and never hope to know, who
the voices I heard belonged to, just that they had
much to say and had finally found someone
hollowed-out enough to listen.

SEASON OF THE SONNETS

For six months I lived inside them.
Stray lines floated up
when I rose early to catch the bus
to catch the train to catch
the other bus that took me to my job.
Like as the waves
make toward the pebbled shore...
or when I lugged clothes
to the laundromat,
That time of year thou mayst
in me behold, or walked with my backpack
through the snow down to Bread & Circus
to load up on sunflower seeds and yogurt.
When yellow leaves,
or none, or few, do hang...
All those weeks and months in my drab costume
of broke twenty-something substitute teacher,
a girl who cut her own hair
in the bathroom mirror and all the while his words
were glints of gold
in my mindstream: *In sequent toil*
all forwards do contend... Five nights a week
I climbed winding stairs
of an old church in the Back Bay
to arrive finally
at the topmost attic under the eaves
where along with a dozen other actors
we'd dive into the sonnets,
make them come alive
like little plays, which is what
they are, glistening fishing nets
cast nightly into the infinite.
And we left everything else
at the door: illness, bad bosses, divorce,
because theater is a temple,

and you don't enter a temple
with shit on your shoes.
So we'd warm up, then turn
to the poems, those "little songs,"
vowels and consonants and diphthongs
sliding over lips, teeth, palate and tongue,
till we broke each word down
to its dulcet syllables. Speaking gibberish,
singing the sweet debate,
parry and thrust, marry or die,
marry and procreate and live forever
in language. All that March and April
I'd walk over the Mass. Ave bridge
from Cambridge into Boston to save the fifty-cent
bus fare, looking down at the Charles River
where Harvard students sculled, privilege
gilding their shapely muscles,
and his lines would float up: *Consumed with that*
which it was nourish'd by....Enchanted
melancholy season when I had
no boyfriend and Shakespeare was my lover,
no stable work, but Shakespeare
was my job. I loved him
the way a Christian loves Jesus,
and I never lost my religion either,
as decades later I find
one or two or sometimes
a whole glittering seam of his words
still shining in my rock-strewn mind,
compressed to diamonds by the weight
of love and time.

TAKE ANOTHER LITTLE PIECE OF MY HEART!

It's 1975 and I have the requisite frizzy hair
and hand-patched jeans, and thrift store velour jacket
and cracked little teenage heart,
and I'm wailing along with Janis to "Me and Bobby McGee"
in my parents' suburban living room
and we're singing *Somewhere near Salinas, Lord,*
I let him slip away, though I have no idea where Salinas is,
or what it means to let someone slip through your fingers
like water or gold dust
and I never knew you were allowed to scream
the way she does on *Take it! Take another little piece*
of my heart now baby! so I try that too,
though I lack her Texas twang, also her full-throated sexual
understanding of what it is to be a woman
who has stripped her very flesh off for a man
who will never love her back
like she deserves. When Janis sings
the song comes through her like a tornado,
violent and perfectly formed,
and I am a clumsy kid with a shaky grasp of pitch
and no idea how to move forward
into a womanhood I can't yet see.
A few years later I'll find myself hitchhiking across Canada
with a man-boy nursing a drug problem,
and we'll jostle along in the cabs
of long-haul truckers down lonely highways
all across the continent. I'll escape him
in Vancouver and get a ride down to California
where I live now, while he goes to pick apples
in the Okanagan Valley, before killing himself
a few years later in the far corner
of a frozen sheep meadow.
By then I'll have an inkling of the thousand ways
life can break a person. I'll listen to Janis
turn herself inside out, going right to the edge
of losing it, and then landing the note anyway,
her voice raw grit streaked with blood,
and I'll have a glimmer of a clue by then,
I'll sink to my knees and bow my head.

Eva Cassidy Live at Blues Alley

She had a cold and didn't think she sounded good,
but it was the only night they were able to record,
and she'd scraped together all the money
she'd been able to save
from her day job in a tree nursery, so they had to go ahead
and use it and now
it's what we have left of her,
and it's live, and it's still happening,
here, in my beat-up little Honda,
decades after her death,
where I'm listening to her sing "Fields of Gold"
like she knows that she won't last the year,
because the wistful way she's conjuring
those fields of barley
where she's promising we'll walk someday,
fools no one. To listen for that blue note
under the melody could shatter you
but you have to let it
pierce the place in your heart
where you've been pretending you'll never die.
That's what I hear anyway,
stopped at a red light
while some joker who doesn't use his turn signal
almost T-bones me. I know
when the song's over she'll leave the stage
too soon. Still the clear strains
continue, even though those fields
are doomed to be buried in snow,
and the lovers parted a few
short months from now.
Because this kind of truth lives on and on—
it is made of silver
                    and light
                            and bone.

PINK SUEDE BOOTS

Decades old now,
but the leather's held up, and the curve
of the instep's still elegant.
I gave them away to my goddaughter, sixteen
and blossoming. She was thrilled.
They're *retro*, they're *vintage*, as I am now,
who once strode the city in my invincible body,
clack-clacking over Cambridge cobblestones
on those sassy kitten heels
like the Princess of Everything.
Resilient relics from another life,
they outlasted a cross-country move,
a starter marriage, and a few bouts of plantar fasciitis,
then languished in my closet for years
until I decided, *Let her have them*,
this girl who is even now stretching toward love
in all its many-splendored disguises
like the limbs of the magnolia in April,
aglow with blushing petals.
And when I say they're *pink*,
let me be clear: not hot pink, nor bubblegum,
but a dusty rose, the color of desire
and rue, color of the secret
places inside a woman
who's been around the block a few times
and knows she's had her share, yet still
wants more—to become what I was
destined to be
before this burning world
had its way with me.

Ballet

The ER doctor finally enters our room
at two a.m. along with a male nurse
and a tech and they cluster around my husband's bed,
to examine his broken wrist. We tell them again
that he's a musician who needs his hands
and the doc's face glows as he lets us know
he plays trumpet, then the nurse shoots my husband up
with more painkillers, and all segue
into well-rehearsed choreography:
one man leans on a bicep, while another pushes a shoulder
deeper into the bed and the doctor takes
my husband's injured hand very gently
in his own as if they were dancing together, which
they are. Four men in a precise and intricate ballet;
the surgeon twists and pulls
puzzle pieces of carpal, scaphoid and trapezius into place,
then tapes up his handiwork with a long fiberglass strip,
weirdly reminiscent at this ghost-hour
of ribbons wound around a ballerina's slender ankle.
My husband, a little high on shock and painkillers,
cracks jokes while they do this thing
that will—please God—keep music streaming
through his fingers a little longer,
but I'm still dazed, my mind full of black ice
on which the car of our old life has just slid
out of control. Oh, to come to earth
to live in a body that breaks, that is destined
to be broken! I'm a mess,
but I do recognize art
when I see it, I recognize devotion,
even here, even now
in this dim theater with no applause.

BOY WITH STOLEN BEGONIA

Breakfast at the outdoor cafe, with Julie.
Begonias in big cement planters
line the entryway; pink, coral, scarlet.
I don't know why it comes out just then, over coffee and eggs,
my sorry confession. *Grief over never having children*
surfaces sometimes like a great gray whale
and swamps my small canoe.
She sips her juice and nods; what could anyone say?
That's when the dark-eyed toddler
wanders to our table, clutching the stem of a torn-off begonia
in his damp baby fist. He heads straight to *my* seat
as if appointed. Gazes into my face.
Hands up his precious offering. I take it.
A minute later, he's back like a well-aimed arrow.
Not to lovely, motherly Julie, who has a son,
but to me. This time he raises his arms up up up
in the universal gesture.
All my well-worn stories stop
in that moment. Everything stops,
except the rip and thud in my chest
as I bend to lift him. Okay, I am greedy
and full of despair. God knows that.
God knows everything.
That's why She sends him to me
a third time, clutching the stem of yet another
torn-off and stolen begonia.
Which he bestows in my palm,
like a blessing, before his mother
scoops him up, laughing, *Sorry he disturbed you!*
And carries him off, leaving me
with a clutch of wilted flowers by my napkin,
and the sound of a something breaking apart—
sticks, old snow, decades of debris—
inside my surging heart.

ELLA, SCATTING

I can't paint the spots on a ladybug's back
or capture the radiance of a cloud of fireflies.
I can't describe what Ella does, if I listen
to her do it a thousand times which I have.
I'm just a mere mortal singing along,
trying to catch up to her swing,
a nanosecond too early, a breath too late.
Sometimes you run for the bus
as it's pulling out of the stop and someone
yells to the driver
and you climb aboard panting.
Sometimes it leaves you
to wait on an empty street
for an hour or the rest of your life.
Then there's Ella, scatting
like a girl playing hopscotch
up and down the scale, so effortlessly,
so joyously, so definitively,
that what can one do
but point: *holy brilliance,*
where did you come from?
Even if it all goes by too quickly
to fathom, the way light
flickering through a prism
breaks and scatters in rainbows
the cat chases to no avail.
Might as well chase your own tail.
Might as well hang out in slack-jawed awe
at the way one scrappy sperm
manages to make its fated rendezvous
with a singular egg,
or a flock of starlings rises all together
in swooping figure eights,
Or a homeless, motherless girl in a dirty dress
climbs onstage at the Apollo,
opens her mouth and lets the whole galaxy pour forth.

DEAR MONSTER

When she does the aria from *Norma*, "Casta Diva,"
she stands still as a willow tree for long moments
through the overture,
arms wrapped around her newly-slender body,
jewels trembling at wrists and throat.
Then smiles demurely as the orchestra swells,
her long almond eyes uptilted,
as if she held a beautiful secret close.
Watch how she waits. Like an animal
who hides her claws for the pounce.
Then when that voice finally comes on
in sinuous waves, its amber beauty
is almost unbearable, but she bears it, she births it
through her wide, avid mouth
which is shaped like the prow of the Argo
carrying Jason and his men away
after they'd stolen the golden fleece.
Oh mouth of Callas, dazzling orifice,
pouring out glory and rue
in sonorous round notes! Oh, lonely workhorse,
exile on the island of fame, who gave everything for Art
and like Medea, trusted faithless men
only to be abandoned in the end. Haven't we all
heard the myths and shuddered, seeing ourselves,
the enraged, ugly outcast,
who transforms herself through sheer force of will,
but even that is not enough.
Art is art. Love is love.
Dear monster, dear sister, *la Divina,*
I have been lonely too. But no one
has been quite as
lonely as you.

Love Warrior

In the hard months after I'd split from my first husband
there were times when I could not bear
to listen to music at all and especially not
to Tuck & Patti, and my favorite
album of theirs, *Love Warrior,*
with its refrain: "We give up on Love
so easily..." because Patti Cathcart's voice
always sounded like it had been soaked
in the dark rum of requited passion for a thousand years,
whereas I'd been stripped down to the bones
of myself, and they were bare, honey,
they were dry as unbuttered toast,
so whenever I heard that song
I'd find myself in a sodden heap on the floor.
But Patti's voice was an infusion,
a womanly call to rise
and face life's ever-shifting modes,
syncopation of the sublime against a backbeat
of the real; the tune I needed to hear
with my whole shattered heart.
You can't put that kind of art
on a staff with notes and a treble clef.
Who knows where it came from, what battlefield
she had to stagger through to sing it
clothed in a faith I could only let enter me
through osmosis, praying that someday its sultry echo
might find me on my feet again.

CLOUDBURST

The loquats ripen, the neighbor's tree
weighed down with clusters of yellow fruit
like ugly Christmas ornaments.
I steal a handful each time I pass.
Two little girls giggle madly
from their perch on a porch.
Yazmin y Isolde.
Black hair, white teeth, they assail me
in Spanish: "Why are you always walking
back and forth, back and forth?"
Por aqui, por acqua.
Trilling their r's perfectly
like mynah birds. I can't do that.
They're the detective-inspector-watchdogs
of our block, keeping a sharp eye out
for scooters and scofflaws, pit bulls
and feral cats. I don't know enough Spanish
to say, *I'm obsessed with my Fitbit,*
and need to get 10,000 steps by nightfall,
so I say "Ejercicio," stumbling
over the consonants, and move my arms like a manic
aerobics instructor which cracks them up.
Their wild laughter is a cloudburst,
it goes on and on
until they're laughing just for the hell of it,
a waterfall of mirth, soaking me down to my sneakers
and sweat-plastered t-shirt.
They are twin warrior-queens who rule this joint,
and I'm just a graying shadow, like most adults.
Their smiles gleam
like undiscovered galaxies. Oh fierce
and fiery girls, go forth and eat the world.
You can start with me if you want.

"Insatiable"

He said it like it was a good thing,
and it did sound better in Spanish:
"In-sat-see-ah-blay."
We twisted together like eels
in the dampened sheets,
lay together afterwards,
sweating, breathless, happy,
but decades later the term haunts me
with its echo of desolation.
Because even in afterglow
there was still the ache.
Which was how I knew
myself to be alive, but still—
that hunger repelled
unwary swimmers who ventured
out beyond the buoy lines
to my dark lair, and I
don't blame them—it repelled me too,
though I was harbor and hideout,
insomniac incubator
of that ancient reptile other-self,
sea-creature of horror movie fame
who ate and gorged and writhed
within me, and somewhere
in my gut is twisting still,
thickened with age now, barnacled,
monstrous—at bottom, as I said,
where our small vanities, once planted
carelessly, grow—there's the Void.
And now, after The Thing
has eaten its fill, and swallowed
so much love in its gaping maw,
what's left? Nothing but to allow
myself to be swallowed whole
by the story

I myself have told. And remember my former
appetite, what a festival
it was, how I laid everything on that altar
for the ever-hungry gods.
How I fed them for a spell.

FISHBOWL

My friend who was out dancing the Saturday night
before everything changed,
stepping and spinning and dipping the ladies,
said the lockdown caught him by surprise.
I felt like a fish that was swimming happily in the ocean
that someone scooped up in a net
and plopped into a little fishbowl,
and I've been swimming in circles ever since,
banging up against that cold hard glass.
We're walking by the marina six feet apart, his hair
grayer than I remember, mine too I'm sure.
Boats on their moorings; sea-beaten pilings.
"I want a house by a lake," I say. "Where I can just
roll out of bed in the morning and go down to the water."
"Now you're talking," he says,
which means we both know this will never happen.
But to be human is to be a monkey
with her paw caught in a jar of gilded peanuts,
stubbornly refusing to let go of anything—
not the old life which is surely
gone forever, nor of hope,
that half-wrecked container ship, laden with history
and dreams and plague-ridden rats no one knows about,
still chug-chugging toward the open harbor.

I Fall to Pieces

We're singing "I Fall to Pieces," Lee at the piano
harmonizing with me on the chorus,
and what happens to my heart in that moment
as I watch him belt out *You want me to act
like we've never kissed* for all he's worth,
his lashes squeezed tight, so light
they seem silver, his throat open
and unguarded, his naked voice mingled with mine,
is written only in a book whose pages
are never turned by human hands,
whose print appears as radiant ions.
I'm staked to the melody,
while he twists over and under those notes
we know so well having practiced them
a million times, and we're doing it, we're going
to pieces together, not like Patsy Cline,
whose heavenly alto was silenced forever in the woods
where the small plane she was taking
to her next gig crashed, but like two old fools
helplessly besotted with each other, and the words
I'd go to Hell for that man arise inside me unbidden,
and scare me half to death because I know
they're true and I know what they mean—
I've seen the wife of the man with Parkinson's
feed him oatmeal, interpret his grunts and moans,
when no one else can understand
what keeps her tied there
letting her own life gutter in his sputtering flame.
I've listened to parents who dragged their kid to rehab
over and over until it stuck, though they had to take out
a second mortgage on their house.
And I've already gone to hell for him
in small ways of course, like he's done for me,
through depressions and dry spells
and bad bosses and illness, but it's the walk
through the valley of the shadow

I'm talking about here, though in truth
I can't imagine it, I just know if he dies
before me, I'll follow
the sweet echo of this moment
to the underworld like Orpheus,
and the whole way down I'll be singing our song.

My Vibrato

My singing teacher says uncontrolled vibrato
is insecurity wearing a frilly blouse,
like the upspeak of a nervous student
peppering everything she says with *kind of* and *you know*.
He says commit to each note like you mean it,
and I agree, I want to make a pure tone
without apology or wavering,
or bleating like a nanny goat, but oh,
as I ascend past G and then A into the attic
of my upper register I feel things begin to throb
and not in a good way.
Here comes my vibrato
like a teetering pile of red Jell-O,
or a drunken ex-girlfriend at the wedding,
smeared lipstick and too much perfume.
And yes, I'm embarrassed to be wobbling around
like a little girl wearing her mother's high heels,
but doesn't everything on earth
vibrate with a mortal shudder?
Candle flickers, moonlight shivers the pond,
and even long-dead stars
pulsate in their inky firmament.
It's only the angels who do not sweat or bleed,
whose pudenda are smooth as Barbie dolls,
whom you'll find singing hosannas forever
each note steady as a laser beam,
never trembling or flinching.

Vibrato Ghazal

Like a trembling tower of fruity gelato,
ladies and gentleman—my vibrato.

Even though my voice teacher says not to
warble like a church lady, my vibrato

blurs the pure tone, a little rubato
(how we hate to be confined!)—because my vibrato

has a mind of her own, even sotto
voce you can hear the tremulous vibrato.

Like a wren chirruping to her inamorato—
hard to quell that pesky vibrato.

Or an operatic artiste, alone in her grotto,
practicing arias, throbs forth the vibrato.

Lee, glancing at this notebook, asks if I sought to
write an ode to my vibrator? No, babe! My vibrato!

Sing smooth as honey, that's my motto,
but there she goes again! Vibrato, vibrato.

BEING WRONG

One of the great
unheralded joys
of late middle age
is the mind-popping sensation
of how many things
I've been wrong about,
starting with the meaning of the word *bruschetta*,
then gliding on seamlessly to men,
marriage,
and magic mushrooms.
All my firmly held opinions
have loosened
like teeth in receding gums
or pilings that the indifferent sea
has pounded into submission.
What a relief to have been wrong
about gluten-free pasta
and skinny jeans,
gender and white privilege!
I suspect I've been mistaken
about pretty much everything,
including death,
which will come for everyone someday,
except me.

MUSIC WE MAKE IN THE BASEMENT

You ask if I can sing the four-note bass line
over and over, and I do, I'm proud
of how low I can go these days,
now that age has deepened my girlish soprano
into the dark earth.
And then I hear you, softly at first,
singing high above me in fluted falsetto,
and it's thrilling because we always laugh
about your five-note range, but this
is a treble surprise you've pulled out of the ether!
I keep up the low thrum, as instructed,
perhaps I have become an insect,
a beetle or a grasshopper,
or maybe I'm making the sound trees make
in the privacy of the forest,
their deep wooden mating calls.
Years ago we tried and failed to harmonize,
but here we are now: I've learned how to anchor myself
to the beat, you to let go and soar,
an intimate reversal.
Back in the day my friends and I
would joke that a deep resonant bass
could shiver our lady parts—
Barry White! we'd moan,
giggling, and mock-fainting—and it's true
I feel that gentle growl
vibrate my own pelvic bowl,
but tonight your clear soprano notes
are what's doing it to me baby, so go ahead,
you be the high-flyer, I'll hold down the root
just like this for as long as we want.

II

Holding Vigil

Holding Vigil

—three days before the 2024 election

My cousin asks if I can describe this moment,
the heaviness of it, like sitting outside
the operating room while someone you love
is in surgery and you're on those awful plastic chairs
eating flaming Doritos from the vending machine
which is the only thing that seems appealing to you, dinner-wise,
waiting for the moment when the doctor will come out
in her scrubs and face-mask, which she'll pull down
to tell you whether your beloved will live or not. That's how it feels
as the hours tick by, and everyone I care about
is texting me with the same cold lump of dread in their throat
asking if I'm okay, telling me how scared they are.
I suppose in that way this is a moment of unity,
the fact that we are all waiting in the same
hospital corridor, for the same patient, who is on life support,
and we're asking each other, Will he wake up?
Will she be herself? And we're taking turns holding vigil,
as families do, and bringing each other coffee
from the cafeteria, and some of us think she's gonna make it
while others are already planning what they'll wear to the funeral,
which is also what happens at times like these,
and I tell my cousin I don't think I can describe this moment,
heavier than plutonium, but on the other hand,
in the grand scheme of things, I mean the whole sweep
of human history, a soap bubble, because empires
are always rising and falling, and whole civilizations
die, they do, they get wiped out, this happens
all the time, it's just a shock when it happens to *your* civilization,
your country, when it's someone from *your* family on the respirator,
and I don't ask her how she's sleeping, or what she thinks about
when she wakes at three in the morning,
cause she's got two daughters, and that's the thing,

it's not just us older people, forget about us, we had our day
and we burned right through it, gasoline, fast food,
cheap clothing, but right now I'm talking about the babies,
and not just the human ones, but also the turtles and owls
and white tigers, the Redwoods, the ozone layer,
the icebergs for the love of God—every single
blessed being on the face of this earth
is holding its breath in this moment,
and if you're asking, can I describe that, Cousin,
then I've gotta say no, no one could describe it
we all just have to live through it,
holding each other's hands.

At First

At first it was that the hostages looked like kinfolk,
their curly hair, dark eyes always saying
three things at once, their smiles
with that undercurrent of anxiety bubbling beneath.

It's that I placed myself among them.

My people, famously stubborn, yes, stiff-necked survivors
slogging through history as sandal-shod refugees,
wagon-pullers, chicken farmers, Torah scholars,
people of ten thousand opinions. At first it was that,

because family is the cauldron I was cooked in, Jerusalem

the direction I was taught to turn my heart.
Then it was my friend who called me, sobbing,
"Why does the world hate us?" or my other friend
who wailed "Where does this end?" or the stone

in my own heart, heavy, never to be dislodged.

Same stone I'd been carrying for thousands of years.
But as the days bled into each other and I bore helpless witness
to the plagues rained down in my name on those we called *other*,
when I saw that the soft bodies of children were the battleground,

the stone began to burn with rage and then shame,

because suffering does not ennoble,
and every people has been chosen,
and Jerusalem is a crossroads and a crucible
and a test of humanity we have thus far failed to pass.

Winter Solstice 2024

Leslie and I walk around the lake,
talking, talking. Post-election, pre-takeover,

Oakland looks the same, but shimmers
with mortal radiance—this world

we thought we knew is vanishing. We pass the guy
on rollerblades skating backwards,

and the woman in a hijab, pushing a stroller.
No pelicans today. Plenty of mallards.

Homeless encampments on the great green lawn.
When we circle back to the pergola, the drums are so hot,

dancers have stripped off their shirts.
One flips upside-down, hopping on a single sinewy arm.

Another carves the flight of birds with his torso.
A baby enters the circle and bounces up and down

like a pogo stick that can't quite get airborne,
the shape of her diaper visible beneath tights

printed all over with black-and-white hearts.
An old woman, regal in robes of kente cloth

and leaning on her cane, steps into the circle, rocks
in time, two-steps with the baby who is soon

holding one end of her cane as the drummers
multiply, a small crowd quietly gathering.

And while the country is getting ready to goose-step
off a cliff, and we know, come summer, we may be masked,

and choking on smoke, still, this is our town,
our state, golden even in winter, even broke, uninsurable, aflame,

we are here now, shoulder to shoulder, all
races, all ages—and I know how corny, how "woke"

this sounds, there is no other way to say it—
watching the dancers, the drummers nodding to each other
in the ever-widening circle, and doing
what they do, which is to stop time

or at least suspend it a moment,
so we can see it shimmering—

and the old lady and the baby are still at it,
having been joined by a shimmying

assortment of others, moving, dancing, singing
while the brief sun sets in a pool of its own reflection,

resplendent amid the broken clouds of evening.

PRAISE THE BROKEN PROMISE OF AMERICA

Praise deep mineral veins under rich dirt,
and fossilized remains of dinosaurs turning themselves into gas
for our benefit. Praise the exhausted earth,
miles and miles of subsidized corn
and cattle lowing from their hell-holes
in automated milking barns.
Praise farmworkers rising before dawn,
their sore backs and aching knees. Praise the myths
that drew them here, stories eagerly consumed
when there is nothing to eat but faith.
Praise the courage of the reverend to look
the dragon in the eye and preach mercy;
praise whatever hidden waterways are still pristine.
Praise music that refused to play at the funeral of democracy.
and the killing cold that swept through Washington
when the fake Pope took power.
Praise drag queens and lipstick lesbians, boys who are girls
and girls who are lions, butch women wearing tool belts,
and all the music theater nerds
who are even now building new passageways
mapping the next underground railroad
and suiting up to be conductors—oh, everybody,
get on board! This train will chug quietly
across the great plains and over rocky Sierras,
into the desert where people still leave bottles of water
and packets of food for the desperate
who have always been the lifeblood
of this nation. It will stop in obscure hamlets
to pick up fugitives with tears tattooed on their cheeks
and fraying backpacks overspilling with contraband books.
Praise the weirdos because if anyone can save us
it will be us. And praise all the glittering illusions
we gawked at, ignoring our own neighbors
in favor of a 24-hour peep show on the Internet.
Praise the convict fire fighters on the front lines in L.A.,
battling the insurmountable for ten dollars a day. We gambled

our future for a hot air balloon with a hole in it. Praise
our reckless hubris, and the infinite distractions
of the hall of mirrors we find ourselves in now, and bless
our overwhelmed brains, scurrying like mice for shelter.
Bless our collective rage, and protect
the officers who stood up on January 6th and now see their attackers
roaming the streets like rabid dogs, ah, bless the animals
we have always been, in our coats and shoes
and clumsy language, bless our willful ignorance,
so enormous, so world-altering, that, like the great wall of China,
it can be seen from outer space,
where the gods are shaking their heads even now,
in pity and in awe.

I REMEMBER FREDDIE

who always hung out on High Street
lounging against his Chevy,
asking for hugs. He used to catch me
as I walked home from mailing a package,
and I'd gamely enter his leather-jacketed embrace
with only a fraction of a second's hesitation
that I'm sure he felt. My hair
would brush his cheek as I inhaled his scent
of pomade and cigarettes.
Last time I saw him was early days
of the pandemic, when the plague
was just becoming real, as in real to *us*,
and I was scared, we all were.
It was some unknown
shadow, hovering over us like a hawk
over a field full of mice, taking his time
to select a victim, Freddie opened his arms
as usual, and I backed away.
"I can't hug you," I said.
"Aw, that Covid business ain't nothing,"
he insisted, arms still open like a little kid,
and when I said no again,
he followed me into Brookdale Park,
until I scrambled up a muddy embankment
in my terror to get away.
What does a hug cost, what's it worth in the end?
People have died for less. But I wasn't ready
to risk it. And now I haven't seen him
in ages, nor that old red car of his
that was always parked
opposite the funeral home,
its back seat stuffed with black,
spilling-open trash bags, radio turned up,
bestowing smooth jazz for free
on any passerby.

Accompanying My Friend to Chemo

She shows me how she draws in her missing eyebrows
with the little make-up kit they give out—
two umber arches
over wide, dark, expressive eyes;
then sparkly earrings, some lip gloss,
a soft fleece cap over her bald head,
and bunny socks.

In Oncology, hooked into her port-o-cath,
blue chemicals dripping from a bag,
she asks the nurse how she's doing,
how's the situation with her car.

Across the room a radiant woman in a headscarf
sits smiling, surrounded by daughters.
This is what's happening
all over the world,
bald, beloved women minus their breasts
holding faith together in the chemo den.

And it's not good literary technique to say
that women's bodies are battlegrounds
in a war we did not start.
It's not artful or ironic and it doesn't begin to tell
this intimacy. But here we are, anyway,
sipping tea, flipping through "People" Magazine,
letting the hours slip by like slow honey.

A FEW DAYS AFTER MY FIRST VACCINE,

walking around Lake Merritt,
I lose an earring
and don't even notice it at first,
overwhelmed as I am
by the new strangeness of everything.
Blocks later, I felt it, miniscule
imbalance, strange lightness in one lobe.
So then I have to retrace
my steps, past the guy jogging
with his mask pulled down,
and the hijab-wearing,
stroller-pushing young mother in stylish jeans,
and the homeless man emerging from his tent
bearing a boom box on one shoulder.
And that's where I spot it, lying on the sidewalk,
miraculously untrampled—small, precious
found thing, a turquoise oval
encircled with rows of beads,
given to me with love by someone
I haven't hugged in more than a year.
Tiny rescue from the sea of loss,
just as we seem to have found
a raft to grab on to
in the wake of a shipwreck so vast
we cannot yet imagine the end of it.

Good News

There are times when the worst
thing you could imagine
doesn't happen. The eggs left boiling in the pot
until they're smoking fireballs,
and the pot itself a blackened shell,
doesn't burn the house down.
You get there in time to open the windows,
run cold water, laugh
at yourself and shake your head.
Your family, it turns out,
has loved you all along, more than you knew,
despite your baffling inability
to get with any sort of program.
It is possible to learn to embrace your fate,
as Joseph Campbell says,
though he doesn't tell you how.
Sometimes you stumble but don't fall.
The bees are making a quiet comeback,
sweet-talking the bougainvillea blossoms,
and the hummingbird has built her thimble nest
on an impossibly skinny twig of the peach tree,
so small your husband has to point at it
for five full minutes: *There! There!* while you peer
out the smudged windshield of your glasses until
the branch moves and you see her,
ensconced on her tiny throne,
breasting the breeze like a figurehead.

BISCUITS

Husband's got a cold, so I make him biscuits—
flour, buttermilk, salt, and he thanks me
over and over. It's so easy
to make him happy. My friends and I used to joke
about men, that they don't need much, just food
and touch, whereas *we* complicated creatures…
I even had a therapist tell me *Women*
are always wondering
what men are thinking—it's a waste
of your time! They're not. The onion
when peeled, is just another
dumb bulb. But I have known
a little something of the male mind,
its loneliness and ghosts, its tangled underbrush. Still,
on this winter afternoon the smell
of risen biscuits fills the house,
and I find myself simply happy
to be animal and mated
with another of my species,
living side by side
with this strange creature, the warm
flannel-shirted length of him, his fingers
at the piano weaving harmonies
that shouldn't work together but do,
his book splayed open on the coffee table,
lost reading glasses roosting on top of his head.

Manicure

Chipped, peeling magenta, glossy as a new car,
incongruous on my aging peasant hands,
still shines bravely
a week after my teenage niece,
who insisted we go to the salon together,
has flown back home with her boyfriend.
What remains of their visit is memory, residue,
trickles of sand from our trip to the beach.
I confess, I like my bedazzled talons,
the way they gleam and sparkle
as I wash dishes or dig in the garden,
further ruining what's left of their sheen.
My niece, lovely in her satin skin,
floated through her days here with a grace
I never had at her age. Who knows
what she and her boyfriend
thought of my husband and me—lumbering
stiffening, sighing, worried old relics
who ferried them to the city's museums and tourist traps,
where they bought matching T-shirts and baseball caps
to commemorate their trip to California?
I remember the elders of my youth:
How they were bit players
in the central drama that was *my* heroic quest.
How harshly I judged them, and also how I envied
their faded battle scars and
that the storms of life were (I thought) behind them.
Plus, as my niece remarked, "When you're old,
you have more money."
I myself am wealthy with regret,
affluent in aching knees and, OK, perhaps
a few things done right,
including the ramshackle remains
of a ridiculous manicure, conceived
and carried out in love.

HARD LISTENING

He's tuning the piano.
Listening hard.
Plink! plink! and then
silence while he considers,
then a tiny pop-skritch-pop
as he adjusts something,
then back to the plinking again.
We've had a heat wave
so everything's gone flat—
the strings, my appetite
for life. Come winter
it'll all contract with cold
and sharpen again,
and next spring
he'll be back at it
with his tuning wrench and fork
and the stop clip
and the little rubber mutes.
I am listening to the intensity
of his listening.
Eighteen years together
and we still work
to hear the wounds
under the words. To listen
purely, the way he is now,
every cell of his body
quivering with attention,
as he leans in
to the upraised lid,
closing his eyes
when the softest hammers
vibrate.

ODE TO BARBRA

Of course I love it that you refused
a nose job—all us girls who were told we too
could be beautiful and loved if only
we weren't, you know, *ourselves,*
owe you for standing up to the knife.
You were afraid it might alter your voice.
I loved your moxie as much or more
than I loved your singing, to be honest;
that dramatic vibrato reminded me of Brooklyn,
each note rich and dripping
with too much expression, the way my Nana and Uncle Sol
would bring us a whole whitefish wrapped in oily paper
twice a year when they visited,
grease leaking through the layers,
embarrassing, redolent, delicious.
Which is how I felt
about the over-the-top-ness of you, Barbra—
who worked around the clock to get
every note just right, sparing no one
least of all yourself
in your quest for perfection.
And you made it!
How many can brag about *that?*
And yeah, I know they say you're a narcissist
and a control freak, they can say
whatever they want, but when I think about the shit
we Jewish girls go through
and I consider how you always knew
you were sexy *and* smart
and had the nerve not to apologize for it,
I contend that it's your right, nay,
your sacred duty to be graced
by flattering lights, to drip with diamonds
and be wrapped in cashmere,
to sing your giddy delight over having survived
through the divine architecture
of your dauntless nose.

JULY AFTERNOON

Not the lovemaking, but the afterglow. The ebb.
Clean sheets on the bed, breeze stirring the curtains.

Not the bliss, but delicious rest, when we're two canoes
moored to the same dock, bobbing in gentle backwash,

you drifting out to dream, me resisting slumber
because I don't want to miss

even a moment of this,
your long warm limbs touching mine,

hip to hip to thigh all up and down the length
of us. And what if we're already dead (I whisper,

knowing you won't hear). What if it's been a thousand years
by now, our house long gone to dust, and this spot

where we're lying is a meadow again,
dotted all over with tiny purple flowers?

JEWEL LAKE, 1994

I used to take the neighborhood kids
up to the Little Farm in Tilden Park,
back in the nineties, after I'd split from my first husband,
and was slowly finding my feet again in the new life.

The cow was massive and calm.
she chewed her cud, she *ruminated*,
extending her long rolling tongue
which was a brownish purple, rutted as an old road.

It terrified five-year-old Patty who clung to my waist
while the goats butted up against the fence, slot-eyed and voracious.
Abraham tickled their noses with long blades of grass.
I told him not to tease them, so he did it some more.

I have no pictures from those days—I didn't
own a camera, and there was no husband or lover
off in the wings, framing shots. No cell phone with which
to snap a selfie, no Facebook to post to and say *Look at us!*

Sometimes we went to Jewel Lake and waded in,
letting minnows nibble the fine hairs on our calves.
No one knew where we were or cared.
I ventured deeper and deeper and stared

at my wavering reflection in green water.
Nothing buzzed or pinged in my pocket.
All was quiet save for the shouts of the children
skipping stones and scaring the fish.

THE BIRD OF YOUR LIFE

The piano is black with white teeth,
like a whale's mouth,
and my nursery school teacher presides over it,
she is the boss of music.
Under her fingers the songs spring up
like wildflowers, and I know them all by heart:
Row row row your boat, and
Here we go 'round the mulberry bush.
When the bright tunes spill
into the messy room, our chaos stills
and even mean Ralphie stops throwing blocks
to listen for a moment.
I'm four and I still see melodies
as bursts of color, swirling in air—
turquoise and orange streamers,
streaks of royal purple. This morning
she has us perched on the little rug,
expectant as a row of trained seals
waiting for our fish.
The game is to guess the name of the tune
from the first few bars, but before even one
of her fingers has touched a single key,
I call out—"In the Good Old Summertime"!
Miss Pamela swivels on her piano bench.
"How did you know—?"
But I don't have words to tell her
that I didn't guess, I *recognized*
the unstruck chord, hovering
like a thought in the air,
like the bird of your life
winging towards you, ready or not.

What kills me about Amy Winehouse

is to see her when she was just starting out,
fresh-faced, goofy, a little shy;
but her phrasing, from the start, impeccable,
and that voice, black cauldron full of inky fire.
Even later when she was drunk
all the time, falling-down,
slurring-her-words drunk, she was still
always on key, still keeping the beat so perfectly,
she could stretch it, spin it, take it for a ride,
she could swerve the limo
of that song across four lanes
of traffic, screeching, tumble out the door—
ripped stockings, bloody knees, beehive—
and the music never stopped
moving through her like a heartbeat,
like the only thing
keeping her alive. Her lyrics were sly
and funny and mean:
"What kind of fuckery is this?"
a question many of us ask ourselves
on a regular basis. Her genius as big
as the lure of the abyss, where she was drowning
in plain sight, pushing all life-rafts aside.
I've got nothing to brag about, I sang along
to "No, no, no," like all the others,
and rubbernecked while she performed
her inevitable demise. How many
never-to-be-written songs
were buried with her that day,
how thick the air now
with their orphan cries.

BLUES FOR BILLIE

You can pick apart a flower and never find its scent—
Tear all the petals off that flower,
You won't know where the magic went.

Elegant as satin, intimate as breath,
My voice wraiths up like smoke rings
Around a slender branch,

Then my vibrato blossoms,
you can hear it float
and gather; hear the tease, the coax

of it—something lightning-struck,
or maybe I just don't give a fuck.
No, it's something tremulous that wants to live

but can't... It draws you closer.
It draws you in.
It says See what they did

to this beauty—
blood in every note,
blood at the root.

You can hear it rising
from the hospital bed
where they've chained me by a slender foot.

NINA

Nina Simone regards the audience at Montreux
with a look that mingles bemusement
and panic, as if she's just been dropped there
from another planet. It's been years
since she fled the States
and a violent husband, in a violent time;
years since she performed *Mississippi Goddam*
and was hounded into exile,
and she's bone-weary from trying to explain
the unspeakable to the deliberately deaf,
but a woman's got to eat, so here she is onstage
in Switzerland, singing
for her supper again with that voice
whose tone ranges, as she herself said,
from gravel to coffee with cream,
her long fingers raining down judgment on the piano,
her phrasing pointedly staccato,
back straight as a Doric column,
muscular shoulders carved out of teak,
every inch classical, strict, erect.
She looks around for David Bowie—
"He is my *friend*," she says,
and you can see on her face
what that means. How few the true
boon companions in this lifetime.
How relentless the battering waves.

KAREN CARPENTER ON TOP OF THE WORLD

My mother pushed the shopping cart at A&P,
buying cream of mushroom soup and canned tuna,
while I stood transfixed in the magazine section,
reading the latest edition of *Tiger Beat*.
The Carpenters were on the loudspeakers,
they were everywhere that year,
like air or water, especially Karen Carpenter,
whose voice was as thrillingly deep and low
as the hush inside a Redwood grove,
smooth as a swatch of velvet held against
your cheek.
The tabloids I read featured full-colored spreads
of her and her brother in their matching Dutch-boy haircuts,
mouths open, singing like celestial twins in perfect harmony.
I never guessed that she was shy
like me, that she would have preferred to hide
behind her drum set rather than be displayed
like an awkward doll. I didn't know she was criticized
for her weight, or that she longed for a life
off the road. Over the years I noticed
how she became thinner and thinner,
collarbones and scapulae jutting out,
but still this seemed to be part of the larger joke
about them, how corny they were, how wholesome, how "good,"
while the real artists were out getting drunk
and trashing hotel rooms. She was truly good, no joke,
she was superb, her voice never cracked or faltered,
no matter the pain, she never hit a sour note.
She just kept crooning, mainlining comfort into our ears,
right to the very moment
she up and disappeared.

UKRAINIAN WOMEN SINGING

If a song could pierce body armor.
If it could penetrate
the enemy's tanks, find them where they sit,
hit their pounding hearts and unshaven faces.
If a chorus of girls in embroidered aprons, arms linked,
were a fierce wind with teeth in it,
or the sharp edge of a knife-blade
held against the invader's throat,
instead of the keening
of women sweeping broken glass
after the bomb blasts shattered the city—
(someone has to do it; someone
has to pick through the rubble).

Wheat fields and fields of sunflowers
cratered with bombs,
and still they are singing.
Grandmothers with broad laps
sing through the bitter night,
their remembered joy
a rough wine—how they once
welcomed the bridal party
with close-braided harmonies.
How they yodeled to each other
from distant hamlets in peacetime
with voices like brass bells
ringing over green hills.

Now their melody gleams and fumes
like gas, and when they hurl
homemade Molotov cocktails
at advancing tanks, they throw
their voices after them,
heave the last of their hearts' fire
at the invaders, other mothers' sons,
because someone has to do it,
someone has to fight to keep singing.

III

Snowy Plovers

ODETTA

She sounded like the ocean,
if the ocean could speak.
That all-encompassing. That deep.
I didn't know it was where she put her rage
until long after I'd learned every note
of *Ballads and Blues* by heart.
It was years before I read her quote:
Folk songs were the anger, the venom,
the hatred of myself and everybody else…
and finally got the whip-crack
that punctuated pathos. She'd found then
an elegant disguise—wrap the wound
in beauty, become a homesick sailor,
or a hungover muleskinner,
back from an all-night jag. Become anyone
other than a complicated woman
singing the ancestors' stories
for crowds of white folk in coffeehouses, at festivals,
then going home to an empty bed.
Criss-crossing the country,
guitar in hand, while reviewers
never failed to mention her "weight."
Yes, she was heavy
with history, the ballast of those thrown
overboard during the Middle Passage,
shackled in iron, ankles and throat. Their voices
demanding release through her genius.
The heft of that grief.
As I said, I knew nothing, I was a teenager
with a cheap turntable and a dozen records
I played over and over,
my tender new self like a baby elephant
trumpeting to the world that someday I, too,
would get to lay my burden down.

RICKIE LEE JONES; LAST CHANCE TEXACO

Waif in a raspberry beret
waltzing up to the microphone
like you've got all the time in the world,
your curled mouth full of mischief and longing.
Bad luck's the soil your voice was seeded from,
sweet and gritty like the last dregs left in the cup.
Soft as a plea—the girl who jumped
or was pushed from the speeding vehicle
and had to limp home, holding her own stilettos
with no one to call. I confess:
I, too, have gotten into cars
where the driver was drunk and stoned and feral.
I, too, have flirted with peril.
Dumb luck we survived being reckless girls
in a feckless time, though luck's
a fickle wind to depend on.
What was it protected us,
when so many others vanished into dust?
You resigned yourself early
to the loneliness that comes
when you can be none other than just yourself.
You kept a stubborn faith that saw you through;
kept your voice true
so we could see your pain and your light,
and like always you're serving up the real thing tonight,
blood-bright and road-weary,
each line a profane hymn,
and we're in your thrall; all
waiting for the end when you lean in
to whisper the mercy shot, the coup de grace,
the answer no one can believe.

ELI'S COMIN', HIDE YOUR HEART GIRL

When I was sixteen and my parents caught me
in the shower with a hapless boy,
my mother berated me through tears,
"It's up to the girl to put the brakes on!"
I had, in fact, been the one with her foot on the gas,
but saying that only made matters worse,
so I was shipped off to Ohio,
to stay with my friend Barah,
temporary exile from the boy whom they hoped
would disappear into the ether,
the way he had after they unexpectedly came home
while I was supposed to be babysitting
the younger kids. But I digress. The problem was
that you can't unfeel what you've felt,
and it had entered me,
not just the boy, but Eros, black-haired god with ruby lips
who creates trouble and bliss wherever he goes.
And then Barah made it all worse
by playing her new record "Eli's Comin',"
hide your heart, girl..., by Laura Nyro,
so I could hear the sound of a woman
in the throes of a passion she can't outrun.
I hadn't had an orgasm yet, and this
was my first hint of what it might be like—that aching,
pleading, reaching, explosive sound
with a hint of gospel thrown in,
because sex is spiritual, and by the end of my stay
I was singing along as best I could,
even the very high parts, because it sounded good to me,
that throb, that ache, that ascent of flying doves
over city rooftops, hell, everything sounded good
in that breaking-open time,
when I was smitten with my newfound Eros,
however ill-aimed his arrows.

"Constant Craving," 1997

I'd set up the room before he came over;
massage table and sweet almond oil,
and k.d. lang's "Constant Craving"
queued up on the boombox.
How he loved the silvery ache in her voice,
the snow-scoured, moonstricken loneliness of it.
He'd joke, afterwards, lying in my arms, a little wistful,
"Are you sure she's lesbian?" "Yes," I'd laugh.
And wonder, privately, about the exquisite surrender
her singing promised, and if I could ever find my way there
with a man. We were a couple of exiles,
him from his home country
where his not quite ex-wife lived with their two children,
me from a marriage that had fissured
under my feet, leaving me crawling through rubble.
So I'm not saying
it was innocent first love between us,
nor the no-holds-barred kind of passion
where you hold hands and jump into the fire together,
Hazmat suits be damned.
More of a tentative shelter we made
from need and tenderness and a well-worn CD
playing her plangent alto over and over.
I remember the freedom
and sorrow of that season
when our bodies asked each other the same
unanswerable question, and how afterwards
white curtains wafted
over the unmade bed.

Canyon

R is steering her way toward a canyon in Colorado—
she warns me we may get cut off—
while I'm circling my neighborhood
like a dog on a leash. Same old ten blocks. She tells me
how a friend of hers, sick unto death
with no cure, chose her own departure date.
R was part of the party that gathered to sing her out,
and all went as planned—still, she says,
it's weird, the aftermath of it,
still sounding inside her.
Death is a mindfuck,
I say, and R laughs so hard
I'm afraid she'll drive right off the road,
and I laugh back, because it *is*,
no matter how much we try, no one
can really wrap their heart around
disappearance. R tells me how her friend
loved the party, how she was singing
up till the very end and I say
That's how I'd like to go,
and she says *Me too,* and there's a universe
of things we could add but don't,
because just then she disappears
into the canyon as forewarned,
her laughter still echoing in the empty air.

Birth

Three a.m. and my friend's been in labor forever;
I'm dozing upright on a stool by her hospital bed.
For hours we've been watching the rim of the skull
crowning between her legs like a black sun
only to get sucked back inside again.
My stomach's growling, and my friend's eyes
are sunk in her head, she's somewhere deep
inside herself, unreachable. The first rays
of what will become daylight begin to seep
through slatted blinds. At seven a nurse brings a tray
of eggs and sausage for her husband.
I wander out to the vending machines
but am too stupid-tired to figure out how to swipe my card.
Clock-time has ceased for all of us, we're floating
in amniotic eternity, like the baby waiting to be born.
The picture of the Virgin Mary
we taped to the wall last night when we were hopeful
for a quick labor, has come undone.
At last the doctor says, *It's now or we'll have to operate,*
and I watch my friend summon the last scrapings
of her strength and push like God on the fifth day
when She created mountains, the whole Sierra Nevada, say—
and still it seems impossible right up to the moment
when all at once, the alien head corkscrews free
of the slit, covered with vernix, and the comma
of the curled-up body follows, unfurling like a sea anemone,
like a flag of the future and it is actually a person, no,
it is *this* particular person—of course, we'd known she was in there
all along, but to see her face as she roots around
for the huge brown nipple—is revelation and genesis and the first
time a human has discovered the world.
I've tried to describe this to anyone who'll listen;
how all of us on Earth have already passed
through the gateway of the impossible just
getting here, and still we don't get it, not really,

and the newspapers are full of plane crashes and market crashes
and the latest outrage, while every single day women
do this thing, they turn their insides inside out
making people out of mucus and milk and hope,
even as the world burns all around us—
and no one, not a single soul, can fathom it.

Including the Hidden Places

The gray-haired woman in the locker room
sits naked on the bench, applying lotion.
Once, long ago, her belly-skin stretched
wide over a baby's head,
stretched and thinned
and never came all the way back,
so there are hills, now, little ripples and folds,
including the hidden places under her breasts,
which droop, like tulips
on the fourth or fifth day,
nodding their heads over the lip of the vase.

A decade after my mother's death
I'm greedily watching this stranger
rub cream into her skin,
its smoothness and swells
and mottled jiggly bits,
its secret pains and pleasures.
I want to speak to her, though etiquette
of the locker room forbids it.
I want her to adopt me, old as I am,
and exhausted from feigning adulthood.
But the world doesn't stop
for such longings. Nothing stops,
including this woman, who pulls on her pants
in silence. In silence I dry off my hair,
zip up my own jacket,
walk out into motherless air.

To a Mother I Know

I have seen you lift
the whole car of your pain
and hold it above your head
with trembling arms.

Seen you bench-press
that two-ton rusted hulk aloft
for eighteen years
so that your daughter

could play in the open air
creating whole worlds, innocent
of the superhuman effort
you were making

to keep the weight
off her. It happens all the time,
mothers do this, they hoist
the unbearable and they bear it,

but witnessing you achieve
the impossible breaks
something in me. Not
my heart but the ice sheath

around it. I think
of my own mother, of course,
and how valiant her effort
at keeping me apart

from her suffering, though you can't
really keep a daughter apart,
we are too much entwined
in one long umbilicus

reaching down
the generations like tree vines.
And this is what's
the matter, mater, mother

of all truths: the weight
of what we try to carry
for each other will never
be fully known.

THE GREAT RIFT VALLEY, KENYA

Behind this scenic overlook
there's a narrow highway full of potholes
on which cars and vans are driving, honking,
swerving, and breaking down.
Also, a little roadside tourist trap,
where against my better judgement,
I've just bought an orange hat
made of tree bark, for twenty-five dollars.
Yes, it's in all the photos,
and looks as ridiculous as it sounds.
The tour bus driver waits patiently
while we snap away with our cell phones,
and shop. Do I need a Maasai blanket
in neon-pink plaid? What about a salad plate
carved in the shape of a hippo?
Or a travel journal made from elephant dung?
What I want is a scent or a whisper,
the ghost of an ancestor
two hundred thousand years old.
Because there's been a rift,
a great rift, between ourselves
and our common mother,
with her populous belly and well-used breasts.
The one who climbed down
from the trees, uncurled her spine
and looked around. Curious,
curious. Picked up a stick
and figured out what to do with it.
Made fire. And from there—
well, it all unfolded as it had to.
We needed to make things, we were compelled
to wander and explore and conquer. Who,
in that great green plain,
shrouded with mist, could have foretold
how far we'd go, how thoroughly we'd forget
where we came from. I forget

for a moment, gazing across the verdant bowl
of this valley, what year it is,
the demented country I call home.
Until the bus tootles,
and sun-screened, tender-footed,
festooned with sunglasses and fanny packs,
we clamber back on board.

The History of Evolution

I'm strap-hanging on the subway,
while a man in a spiked leather jacket
sprawls dead-eyed across a whole seat-bench.
Kids packed too closely next to me are flirting—
with each other, with danger
or the idea of it, with darkness
and its underside. A girl with red lipstick
and precisely ripped fishnets,
makes eyes at the stylish androgyne
lounging on the pole next to her,
then looks away.
She's so close to the other woman,
they're inhaling each other's essences,
yet their talk is determinedly casual,
about some party in the city, their alleged goal.
Now the train shrieks as we enter
the long dark tunnel. It takes forever,
and when we finally stumble off at Embarcadero
we're still us—trudging, shuffling, pawing,
occasionally graceful animals
who smell each other's lust and fear,
who only came down from the trees
and began to walk upright
a million years ago or so—
barely enough time to get started.

AT ALBANY BULB WITH ELAINE

Side by side on a log by the bay.
Sunlight. Unleashed dogs,
prancing through surf, almost exploding
out of their skins with perfect happiness.
Dogs who don't know about fired park rangers,
or canceled health research, or tariff wars,
or the suicide hotline for veterans getting defunded,
or...or...or. We've listed horror upon horror
to each other for weeks now, and it does no good,
so instead I tell her how I held a two-day old baby
in my arms, inhaling him like a fresh-baked loaf of bread,
then watched as a sneeze erupted through his body
like a tiny volcano. It was the look of pure
astonishment on his face, as if he were Adam
in the garden of Eden making his debut achoo,
as if it were the first sneeze that ever blew,
that got me. She tells me how her dog
once farted so loudly he startled himself
and fell off the bed where he'd been lolling,
and then the two of us start to laugh so hard
we almost fall off our own log. And this
is our resistance for today, remembering
original innocence. And they can't
take it away from us, though they ban
our very existence, though they slash
our rights to ribbons, we will have
our mirth and our birthright gladness.
Long after every unsold Tesla
has vaporized, and earth has closed over
even the names of these temporary tyrants,
somewhere some women like us
will be sitting side by side, facing the water,
telling human stories and laughing still.

LISTENING TO "BLUE," 1972

We'd sit on Helen's bed
and play the record over and over,
every note aching with truth,
because those songs were written just for us,
they saw through our ungainly
fourteen-year-old disguise,
to the heart of who we were—
women of the world
who would grow up to break men's hearts
and have our own hearts broken in turn,
until at last we too
would be beautifully sad and wise
as she was, and skate away
toward whatever we imagined
womanhood to be.
Helen with her long brown hair
rippling over her half-hidden face
as she fingered her guitar,
her voice clear and true, and me
always a little shaky, a little off-key,
a little hopelessly in love with her.
But when you're in love, really
and truly, it's your own hejira,
no one to possess or blame,
as Joni Mitchell knew
and told us in her ice-pure, regretful soprano,
the shimmer of her voice
like starlight over new snow,
like we girls, who were shimmering too,
though we were the last to know.

Barbie Manifesto

I'm gonna see the *Barbie* movie tonight
because I had a feminist mother who didn't buy us Barbies
and when I said I wanted to be a nurse, she said why don't you be a doctor,
but I really did want to be a nurse
because of the perky hats they got to wear,
bobby-pinned to their sleek, shiny hair,
and I'm going to wear pink to the Barbie movie,
hot pink, the color of cheap candy,
like the chalky sugar cigarettes we pretended to smoke
with their fake red tips,
and I'm going to squeal like a cheerleader on Ecstasy,
I'm going to be silly and girly and super excited,
and all the things you were never supposed to be,
because doing anything like a girl—running,
or throwing, or thinking or writing or talking,
is the worst insult—
an icky, sticky, oozing, bleeding, shrill, smelly girlie-girl.
It means you're not smart, or cool.
You cry when they throw footballs at your chest
which my boyfriend did in high school
because he wanted to help me toughen up.
It means you'll be laughed at and dismissed,
so I've acted serious and intelligent
and tough for about a thousand years, just to prove them all wrong,
but now I'm begging to be dismissed—please! Dismiss me,
so I can lounge by the pool in a bright pink bikini
while some Ken brings me drinks with little umbrellas.
Because I'm tired of proving my point.
I don't remember what my point is anyway,
or the point of this whole thing in the first place—
men, women, who cares? I just want to hide under the bed
with my best friend and a flashlight, constructing secret worlds
we can live in forever. I want to grow old on Planet Girl,
painting each of my stubby fingernails a different color of neon.
I have pretended I sprang fully-grown
from the forehead of my father, bristling with armor.

I have worn olive drab and camouflaged the delight I once took
in smearing myself with Vaseline and admiring my new little breast-buds
in the midnight mirror. I have done all the right things,
I have feigned interest in what bored me,
I have feigned politeness. I have pretended that my inner organs
are not all glistening pink, my heart and my liver and my lungs.
Pink as your own tongue, or the pads of your feet, or your palms.

City Chickens

They strut around their concrete enclosure, pecking for seed,
like disgruntled old ladies, making a mild fuss

about the food while empty chip bags and soda cans
blow against their rusty chain-link fence.

I have a friend vacationing in Portugal as we speak.
Another touring temples in Japan. Yet another on a tiny island

off the coast of Greece, while I'm marooned here,
counting steps around the same old city block,

exchanging daily WhatsApp messages with my friend,
the one on the island. She wonders if she'll ever settle down,

and if not, is something wrong with her? Probably. I mean,
there's something wrong with all of us. I never thought

I'd end up like this, domesticated as a pet lamb,
with a mate who worries our hundred-year-old house

needs new everything, shingles to foundation.
But such is fate. Oh my sweet, my stick-in-the-mud, my dear,

who still touches my face tenderly
in the kitchen, and knows I'll always hanker

and hunger, whine and sigh over other people's Instagrams. No fix
for an itchy mind. We'll probably never go anywhere

but it's okay (most days.) I've seen Paris. I've been to Peru.
Which brings me back to the chickens.

What neighbor was it sought to create
their dream farm scenario in an East Oakland tenement?

Enclosed by a chain link fence, guarded by a slobbering dog,
the hens pick their way with scabrous claws

over pebbles and cement, emitting soft, gossipy squawks.
They're distant descendants of dinosaurs like all of us,

wearing our ordinary disguise, scanning the world
for food or danger, with hungry eyes.

SNOWY PLOVERS

Winter twilight on Alameda Beach.
Leslie and I watch
a flock of snowy plovers
make figure eights against a slate horizon.

Their wild wheelings trace the shape
of wonder and grief moving inside us,
pewter, then platinum.
It goes away like that; it comes back.
It carves a black, moving river in the air.

A year since Leslie's sister went deep
into the green woods,
where she made her plan and carried it out.
Death the only open door
she could perceive.

For the living who are left, the answer's
indecipherable; a scribble
of bird-wing calligraphy
in dove-gray gloaming.

As we watch, the murmuration turns
and circles back to settle
plump on the sand all together
in a plover convention,
all without a word of consultation,
or any kind of vote,
white breasts gleaming like tuxedo shirtfronts.

Up to our ankles in foaming surf,
we feel the tug of tide pulling back,
while our chilled toes curl
on sucking sand. The world
tilts on its axis. Nothing to hold onto.

A Scrap of Blue

Gray blustery day by the lake.
I'm walking to the bank,
hood up, shoulders hunched
when I pass a woman
watching the tea-colored water.
She's got that look we humans get
when we see a baby anything.
This time it's a tiny coot,
black as wet velvet,
just learning to fish, tipping head down
into the drink, then popping up again
like a cocktail glass ornament.
I wouldn't have seen it on my own,
striding blindly as I always am,
fighting the elements,
fighting late-stage capitalism
and losing. But I could ride
the coattails of her attention
for a moment, could notice
her noticing and so slip
through a crack between
the thousand kinds of oblivion. A scrap
of blue when clouds part
just enough. In twelve step programs
they say you have to be willing,
but if you're not, then perhaps
you might be willing to be willing,
and so on, until finally some kind of light
may find even you, however cranky
and rain-splattered, however far
you think you are from home.

OFFERING

Walking my street at dawn—
another broken bottle smashed
in a neighbor's driveway.
Shards of clear glass
scattered in stars
trembling in first light, tossed
from a moving car
or flung down
by the drinker
at his very own feet.
I look down at the wreckage,
up at a tree,
pink petals pushing
out of bud tips,
then double back home
for broom and dustpan
and begin sweeping.
It takes a long time
to pick the tiniest bits
out of the asphalt,
carrying jagged fragments
back and forth to the recycling.
Who knows why but this
makes me stupidly happy all morning.

ARETHA FRANKLIN: "RESPECT"

"They say you can hear the anointing in the voice."
— singer Jennifer Hudson, who portrayed Aretha
Franklin in the Apple TV series "Respect"

Her voice from the first
carried the strength of a woman, unrehearsed
conviction, forced on a young girl
who lost her mother and bore a child
while still a child herself. Who would choose
to be chosen for that? But when the cup
is passed, you drink what's given,
and a life unfolds. That voice,
a bright spear of faith
hurled from the ramparts of circumstance.
When I first heard "Respect,"
not as a plea but a command,
every hair on my body stood up.
How was a woman allowed
to call the tune like that?
Any songbird can learn the notes,
but anointing's a thing apart.
It's a complicated glory to wear the crown
of Queen of Soul. Because soul's
created by crushing coal
till it becomes diamond. Not everyone
makes it out in one piece,
let alone in exaltation. Not everyone
can carry the burning gift
all the way home.

Jewlia Eisenberg: Disturb the Air

I was thirty before I saw a woman rabbi,
or heard a woman cantor chanting from the bima.
By then I'd left my religion behind, pissed
that it was always the men sitting in front,
men talking, explaining, in charge of everything.
Orthodox Jews believe a woman's voice, raised in song,
is so bewitching it will tempt the spiritual aspirant
away from G-d, down jasmine-scented paths of lust.
We were never Orthodox, but I noticed
how the women I knew were careful not to be too big,
too loud. Because no one likes a bossy yenta,
much less an assertive shrew. And I was too
tall anyway, outspoken, ungainly,
know-it-all. So I tried to control what I could:
rounded my shoulders, slumped
my height, pitched my voice deliberately,
pleasantly low. Enter Jewlia Eisenberg,
whose album notes list "sexsounds"
as an instrument, right next to "percussion" and "guitar."
Whose brazen, bosomy, bodacious yodels ran the gamut
from screech owl to oracle,
avenging angel to silken chanteuse,
and light up every nerve in my heart.
Who disturbed the air with a joyful noise. So yes,
the black-hatted rabbis were right—
this kind of power can upend a world.
It can part the seas and raise the dead.
I was never sure of G-d or goddess, whatever you call it,
but I do believe in Jewlia,
who filled the air with her unleashed yips and moans
that make me feel like I am right inside
the place where it all comes from,
the place we return to in the end.

What I Learned

Back when I had my nose pressed
against the glass window of *singing*
as if it were a palace I could enter
only through the servants' entrance, I'd thought
to be able to do *that,* to open
my mouth and have melody pour out,
shimmering, perfect, would be the key
to happiness. And of course I wanted to be
anyone but myself, clumsy and eager
as a shelter mutt. Even as I learned
how it gutted Billie Holliday to sing *Strange Fruit,*
(yet still she sang it, over and over),
and reckoned what Aretha's childhood cost,
and studied up on Ella's loneliness,
I clung to my young dream, I missed the point.
They'll blast the top off a mountain
to get at a vein of coal.
Scar the earth with mines, dam rivers sifting for gold.
Did I say "they"? Make that us.
So well trained to search for the gleam
of brilliance inside anything
and dig out a seam. Put like that,
singing becomes just another shiny thing
and the lives of girl singers (for the most part)
cautionary tales. It wasn't until I stood
by the piano myself, and quavered and croaked
and reached for high notes that weren't there,
and stumbled my way to beauty
that I learned: singing's made of sweat and spittle,
tears and snot, hot breath,
and the soggy crumb of a potato chip left
in a back corner of your unflossed tooth.
They can extract salt from seawater
and alcohol from beer, but a song can't live
without the human body—lungs, ribcage, naked heart—
or the panting hound dog
of a life that cries inside it.

JUMP

Because my car is twenty years old
and the gizmo that goes *ding ding ding*
when you leave the lights on
has been busted for at least a decade,
I'm always contending with a comatose battery,
always approaching strangers to ask for a jump
in Trader Joe's parking lot
or on a deserted street in the growing dark,
where a man in a python-green Porsche
affixes the red and black alligator clamps confidently
yet incorrectly killing the thing altogether,
resulting in a 10 p.m. call to Triple A,
an hours-long wait at a 7-Eleven,
and a midnight ride sitting in the cab
of a tow truck whose driver has just been dumped
by his wife of eleven years
and desperately needs to talk about it.
These are the adventures you may have
if you tend to leave your lights on, as I do,
at dusk when the light is tricky, the hour
entre chien et loup, between dog and wolf
as the French call it,
when the distracted mind is too full of shadows
to remember what you did just moments ago.
By now I'm an old pro at setting up cables,
fitting black to minus, red to plus,
but I'll never get over the small miracle
of how fast it all works, the spark arcing
quicker than thought
as soon as a benefactor turns their ignition switch;
my own car springing to life again
like Sleeping Beauty after just the right kiss,
the way a smile will ricochet from a stranger's face
to my own, or one kind word retrieve
a flailing soul from the abyss.

TETHER

The reason I can't watch astronaut movies with you
is because there's always a scene when the hero leaves the capsule

to fix something vital, a heat panel, say,
and they're tethered to the mother ship

by just a slender umbilicus made of fiberglass
and desperation, a jerry-rigged bungee cord,

and inevitably something terrible happens, a cloud of space dust
or a chunk of meteorite, and the thing snaps,

hurling our conflicted protagonist into empty space
a human starfish stranded in inky nothingness,

with only the sound of his or her heartbeat thudding
inside the dying spacesuit, and although

there's almost always a rescue,
the crew on the ship and Houston on the ground

somehow plot a Hail Mary trajectory
and catch the errant tumbleweed,

it's such a fraught operation that I can't bear to watch—
what if they fumble?—so I study you instead,

so absorbed in the drama you almost forget to breathe,
and sometimes I feel like I'm the mother ship

keeping you connected to earth, saying *It's eight o'clock,*
stop playing the piano, it's time to eat,

but then in other moments when I'm lost
in my work it's you who tracks me down

from behind the computer, and makes me rejoin
the human race, your arms my landing strip.

And I know there comes a day when one of us
breaks this fraying leash of flesh

and goes tumbling toward the great unknown,
while the other is left holding an empty rein, wondering
where did all the singing go? How frail
the filaments that bind us to this life appear

to me now that I confess; you've been my anchor
all these years, it's the beams of love raying out

from your green eyes that tether me here.

Playlist for *Hard Listening*

I have always worshipped women singers. As a kid, I played Odetta's Ballads and Blues over and over on my little suitcase-shaped mono record player in my bedroom, singing along lustily with her fathoms-deep alto: *"And before I'll be a slave, I'll be buried in my grave..."* Completely inappropriate for a suburban white girl, but it was a different time. Later I fell in love with Carole King, Janis Joplin, Joni Mitchell, and Buffy Sainte-Marie.

My adoration of them was laced with yearning and pain. My own singing was off-key. I was crushed when my third-grade music teacher told me not to sing with the rest of the class. I didn't know what a key was. No one in our family played a musical instrument. From then on, every time I opened my mouth to make music in front of another person, I felt terrified they would discover my shameful secret.

Fast forward through the decades: I continued to sing in the shower. I joined no-audition choruses. I married a musician with exquisitely sensitive ears. And when the pandemic hit, stuck at home together, we began to make music, him at the piano, me singing. It did not go smoothly.

I started taking voice lessons on Zoom. I continue with those lessons to this day. I've spent innumerable hours on ear training, doing scales and arpeggios. I've gotten way better, even if my singing is still a work in progress. And I fell in love with a bunch of other women singers: Amy Winehouse, Eva Cassidy, Jewlia Eisenberg. This time around, my love is laced with understanding — I actually have a clue as to what they're doing and how they are doing it.

Homages to these singers and poems about learning to sing make up the core of the collection of poems in *Hard Listening*. Because as every musician knows, listening is the key. Below are influential songs by the artists I reference directly in the book.

1) Janis Joplin "Take another little piece of my heart!" Janis goes right up to the edge of turning herself inside out when she sings. She screams, she wails, she snarls, she growls, she cries. She goes from vulnerable lost kitten to raging lioness and she holds nothing back. There's no one like her.

2) Eva Cassidy "Fields of Gold" At the other end of the spectrum, Cassidy's voice is crystalline, pure, angelic. She makes you lean in to listen. She is an exquisite artist and had she not died at the age of 32 from melanoma, she would be much better know today (although there is good documentary footage of her on Youtube if you care to look.) Her voice will break your heart.

3) Ella Fitzgerald "How High the Moon" or really anything. Ella sings. She was a genius. You can listen to any song of hers 1,000 times and it still sounds fresh. You will hear new spins and twists and nuances in it. She is evergreen. There's a video of her singing Mack the Knife at a concert in Berlin in 1960 where she forgets the words halfway through and proceeds to do a ten minute freestyle, improvising and scatting like the virtuoso she was that will leave your jaw on the floor. She's untouchable.

4) Patti Cathcart of Tuck & Patti "Love Warrior." I listened to this song so many times after my first marriage broke up. It often left me on the floor sobbing, but it also gave me the strength to get up again. Patti's voice is warm, rich, sweet--and comes from a place of pure love. That love infuses every note and reaches out to heal the listener. You can feel it. It's palpable.

5) Patsy Cline "I Fall to Pieces" The core of Cline's voice is strong and vibrant and emotional with a little bit of that Appalachian yodel in it. 0Even when she's singing about heartbreak--which she usually is--it's the voice of a survivor. There's just an extraordinary amount of life-force that comes through her singing. She feels to me like the unsinkable Molly Brown, but she died in a plane crash at the age of thirty. My husband and I sometimes sing this song as a duet with him on the harmony part.

6) Amy Winehouse "Me and Mr. Jones" I had read the tabloids and thought I knew her story; messed-up drug addict who dug her own early grave. It wasn't until after she was dead that I started really listening to her. She was a brilliant jazz stylist, in complete command of her instrument. Her phrasing and timing are flawless and her lyrics are gutsy and funny as hell. I loved her spirit of defiance even though that was her main obstacle. She was her own worst enemy, but the way the media--and all of us onlookers--feasted on the lurid details without appreciating what an incredible musician she was, is shameful.

7) Billie Holiday "Strange Fruit" What is it about Billie's voice? It's a thousand years old. It has seen everything, felt everything, suffered everything. There's a hurt child in her voice and an old woman. There's a prophet and a seer and a vulnerable creature, who no matter how much cruelty she has witnessed, will not be silenced by her trauma. She sings from the wound at the heart of America. But also from its beauty.

8) Nina Simone "Feelin' Good" Nina Simone said of her own voice that is could go from gravel to coffee with cream, and that is true. She original-ly wanted to be a classical pianist but was rejected from the famous Curtis school of music because of her race. She went on to become one of the most powerful singers of her generation. After she wrote and performed "Missis-sippi Goddam" --and after her friends Martin Luther King and Medgar Evers were killed, and her dear friend the playwright Lorraine Hansberry died of cancer, she went into self-exile in Europe and Africa. A complicated, tor-mented woman, her voice carries every shade and hue and texture of the human experience from love and desire to righteous fury.

9) Karen Carpenter "On Top of the World" As a child, I loved Karen Car-penter's voice. It's unbelievably smooth and mellow, like clouds of whipped cream, thrillingly low, and beautiful. Then I got a little older and learned that she was corny and I was embarrassed for liking her so much. Definitely not cool! But as time has gone on she is being appreciated for the incredible vo-cal artist (and drummer!) that she was.

10) Aretha Franklin: "You Make Me Feel Like a Natural Woman" There's a piercing quality to Franklin's voice that gets right inside you. A triumphant joy that comes from a place of pure spirit. She's inimitable (but Jennifer Hudson

and Cynthia Erivo have done very credible performances of her signature songs.) Her voice could bring the walls of Jericho crashing down. She overcame so much and forged a magnificent life with that voice. I bow down.

11) Jewlia Eisenberg "Dying Bed" I know you probably haven't heard of her, but please, I'm begging you, look up Jewlia Eisenberg and the incredible body of musical work she left behind when she died at age fifty in 2021. As founder and bandleader of Charming Hostess she coined the term "Nerdy-Sexy-Commie-Girly"[11] to describe her genre of music which spans an eclectic range of styles. She was an ethnomusicologist, a bandleader, a composer, an historian, a nerd and a powerhouse singer who could handle a wide variety of styles from gospel to traditional Jewish lament, to Balkan close harmonies and more. Her music is weird and wonderful. I cannot do it justice with my words. Go out and get yourself some Charming Hostess and you'll see what I mean.

Acknowledgments

I would like to thank Leslie Absher, Elaine Beale, Susan Browne, Dorianne Laux, Lee Bates, Cary Barney, Marci Rinkoff, the Ari family, and Zack Rogow for reading and commenting on earlier drafts of many of these poems. Thank you, Mark Burrows and the whole team at Wildhouse Publishing, for lovingly shepherding this book through publication, and to dear Rosemerry Wahtola Trommer who led the way to Wildhouse. Thanks to the whole Luter-clan and the precious web of friends who kept and are keeping me laughing and crying and raging and making art in the face of whatever comes. And special love to all the activists stirring up good trouble and fighting Fascism. This book is for us.

I am also glad to acknowledge, with gratitude, these journals and books in which the following poems first appeared:

"Access Road," "Being Wrong," "A Few Days After My First Vaccine," "Jump," "Pink Suede Boots," "Manicure": *The Sun Magazine*

"Insatiable," "Barbie Manifesto," "Vibrato Ghazal," "Holding Vigil" "Praise the Broken Promise of America": *Rattle*

"Boy With Stolen Begonia," "Fishbowl": *Leaping Clear*

"Season of the Sonnets," "Jewel Lake, 1994": *Catamaran*

"Ghosts": *The MacGuffin*

"Music We Make in the Basement": *Writer's Digest* "Non-Rhyming Poetry Awards" First Place

"Love Warrior," "My Vibrato," "Accompanying My Friend to Chemo" "Eva Cassidy, Live at Blues Alley," "Karen Carpenter," "Canyon" "Good News," "To a Mother I Know": *One Art*

"Take Another Little Piece of My Heart Out!": Anti-Heroin Chic

"Offering": *Anacapa Review*

"The History of Evolution": published in *The Town*, an anthology of Oakland Poets (Nomadic Press, 2023)

"Jewlia Eisenberg": *Lilith Magazine*

"Dear Monster," "Biscuits," Blues for Billie," "Caught": *Ephemera*.

"Ukrainian Women Singing," "Nina" *Main Street Rag*

"Including the Hidden Places": *Pensive*

"July Afternoon" and "A Scrap of Blue": *Shadowplay*

"At First," "Hard Listening," "What I Learned," "Snowy Plovers": *Vox Populi*

"Rickie Lee Jones: Last Chance Texaco" in *Women in a Golden State* (Gunpowder Press, 2025)

"I Fall to Pieces": *Southeast Review*

About the Author

Alison Luterman grew up in a suburb of Boston, the oldest of four children. She had her head in a book from the time she learned how to read, and got hooked on poetry when she was six years old. She is third-generation American, the great-granddaughter of immigrants who were allowed into this country at a time when they desperately needed it. She's the inheritor of that privilege, and she doesn't forget it.

She studied poetry at Emerson College and at UMass Amherst where her favorite teachers were Bill Corbett (Emerson), and Julius Lester (UMass.) She fell in love with Frank O'Hara and the whole New York School of poets, an influence that continues to inform her work.

After graduating, Alison joined VISTA (Volunteers In Service to America) and was sent to Miami where she worked with Haitian refugees, learned Creole, and worked as an ESL teacher and a translator for asylum cases. Returning to the Boston area, she continued to work with the Haitian community for years while attending voodun ceremonies and writing a bad novel.

After she moved to California in 1990, she worked as a freelance journalist, massage therapist, HIV test counselor, harm reduction educator for IV needle using drug addicts, drama teacher, actor in a children's theater troupe, poet-in-the-schools, playwright-in-juvenile hall, and adult education teacher. She began to publish her poetry regularly in *The Sun Magazine*, and has taught at Esalen and Omega Institutes, New College, Holy Names College, The Writing Salon, and writing conferences across the country. Currently she offers one-on-one coaching as well as classes on Zoom.

For many years, Alison performed with the improv troupe Wing It! She had always sung in choruses, but during the pandemic she began studying singing with a teacher and continues to this day. She's in a band with her husband and some friends but they don't have a name and have not as yet played a gig anywhere. They just have fun practicing in the living room.

Her previous books are *The Largest Possible Life*, *See How We Almost Fly*, *Desire Zoo*, *In the Time of Great Fires*, and the e-book *Feral City* (now available on Audible.com.) She has also written a half dozen plays, including two musicals. She can be reached through www.alisonluterman.net.